HARCOURT HORIZONS

North Carolina

North Carolina End-of-Grade Test Preparation

Answer Key

Harcourt

Orlando   Austin   Chicago   New York   Toronto   London   San Diego

Visit *The Learning Site!*
www.harcourtschool.com

To the Teacher

Harcourt Horizons North Carolina End-of-Grade Test Preparation provides the support you need to prepare your students for End-of-Grade tests.

The student test booklet is a series of lesson-by-lesson tests, organized by chapter, that use the content in *Harcourt Horizons* to meet the knowledge and skills objectives specified in the North Carolina Standards of Study. The tests are constructed in a standardized-test format consistent with North Carolina's End-of-Grade Tests. Items may include the use of such graphics as maps, webs, diagrams, graphs, time lines, charts, and tables.

At the end of each unit is a reading passage, which summarizes the content in the unit and will help students develop the ability to comprehend and process social studies content. The questions for this section are built upon a variety of reading comprehension strategies: Identifying the Main Idea and Supporting Details; Sequencing, Categorizing, and Comparing and Contrasting; Summarizing, Generalizing, and Making Inferences; Drawing Conclusions and Predicting a Likely Outcome; Identifying Fact and Opinion and Cause and Effect; and Determining Point of View.

Answer Key

The teacher material in this booklet includes an Answer Key that identifies the objectives addressed by the test items. For quick reference, there is also a Social Studies Curriculum Correlation Chart that tabulates the test items for each objective.

We hope that you find these materials valuable in helping your students begin their preparation for North Carolina End-of-Grade tests.

Series Consultants

Janice Miller
Teacher
School Street Elementary School
Goldsboro, North Carolina

Roger Mitchell
Teacher
Green Hope Elementary School
Morrisville, North Carolina

Candace Whitehurst
Teacher
Timber Drive Elementary School
Garner, North Carolina

Copyright © by Harcourt, Inc.

All rights reserved. No part of this publication may be reproduced or transmitted in any form or by any means, electronic or mechanical, including photocopy, recording, or any information storage and retrieval system, without permission in writing from the publisher.

Requests for permission to make copies of any part of the work should be addressed to School Permissions and Copyrights, Harcourt, Inc., 6277 Sea Harbor Drive, Orlando, Florida 32887-6777. Fax: 407-345-2418.

HARCOURT and the Harcourt Logo are trademarks of Harcourt, Inc., registered in the United States of America and/or other jurisdictions.

Printed in the United States of America

ISBN 0-15-335722-3

2 3 4 5 6 7 8 9 10   082 10 09 08 07 06 05 04 03

Contents

Answer Document 2

Answer Key and Item Analysis 6

**Social Studies Curriculum
Correlation Chart** 11

Page 1
1. Ⓐ Ⓑ Ⓒ Ⓓ
2. Ⓐ Ⓑ Ⓒ Ⓓ
3. Ⓐ Ⓑ Ⓒ Ⓓ
4. Ⓐ Ⓑ Ⓒ Ⓓ
5. Ⓐ Ⓑ Ⓒ Ⓓ

Page 2
1. Ⓐ Ⓑ Ⓒ Ⓓ
2. Ⓐ Ⓑ Ⓒ Ⓓ
3. Ⓐ Ⓑ Ⓒ Ⓓ
4. Ⓐ Ⓑ Ⓒ Ⓓ
5. Ⓐ Ⓑ Ⓒ Ⓓ

Page 3
1. Ⓐ Ⓑ Ⓒ Ⓓ
2. Ⓐ Ⓑ Ⓒ Ⓓ
3. Ⓐ Ⓑ Ⓒ Ⓓ
4. Ⓐ Ⓑ Ⓒ Ⓓ
5. Ⓐ Ⓑ Ⓒ Ⓓ

Page 4
1. Ⓐ Ⓑ Ⓒ Ⓓ
2. Ⓐ Ⓑ Ⓒ Ⓓ
3. Ⓐ Ⓑ Ⓒ Ⓓ
4. Ⓐ Ⓑ Ⓒ Ⓓ
5. Ⓐ Ⓑ Ⓒ Ⓓ

Page 5
1. Ⓐ Ⓑ Ⓒ Ⓓ
2. Ⓐ Ⓑ Ⓒ Ⓓ
3. Ⓐ Ⓑ Ⓒ Ⓓ
4. Ⓐ Ⓑ Ⓒ Ⓓ
5. Ⓐ Ⓑ Ⓒ Ⓓ

Page 6
1. Ⓐ Ⓑ Ⓒ Ⓓ
2. Ⓐ Ⓑ Ⓒ Ⓓ
3. Ⓐ Ⓑ Ⓒ Ⓓ
4. Ⓐ Ⓑ Ⓒ Ⓓ
5. Ⓐ Ⓑ Ⓒ Ⓓ

Page 7
1. Ⓐ Ⓑ Ⓒ Ⓓ
2. Ⓐ Ⓑ Ⓒ Ⓓ
3. Ⓐ Ⓑ Ⓒ Ⓓ
4. Ⓐ Ⓑ Ⓒ Ⓓ
5. Ⓐ Ⓑ Ⓒ Ⓓ

Page 8
1. Ⓐ Ⓑ Ⓒ Ⓓ
2. Ⓐ Ⓑ Ⓒ Ⓓ
3. Ⓐ Ⓑ Ⓒ Ⓓ
4. Ⓐ Ⓑ Ⓒ Ⓓ
5. Ⓐ Ⓑ Ⓒ Ⓓ

Page 9
1. Ⓐ Ⓑ Ⓒ Ⓓ
2. Ⓐ Ⓑ Ⓒ Ⓓ
3. Ⓐ Ⓑ Ⓒ Ⓓ
4. Ⓐ Ⓑ Ⓒ Ⓓ
5. Ⓐ Ⓑ Ⓒ Ⓓ

Pages 15–16
1. Ⓐ Ⓑ Ⓒ Ⓓ
2. Ⓐ Ⓑ Ⓒ Ⓓ
3. Ⓐ Ⓑ Ⓒ Ⓓ
4. Ⓐ Ⓑ Ⓒ Ⓓ
5. Ⓐ Ⓑ Ⓒ Ⓓ
6. Ⓐ Ⓑ Ⓒ Ⓓ
7. Ⓐ Ⓑ Ⓒ Ⓓ
8. Ⓐ Ⓑ Ⓒ Ⓓ
9. Ⓐ Ⓑ Ⓒ Ⓓ
10. Ⓐ Ⓑ Ⓒ Ⓓ

Page 17
1. Ⓐ Ⓑ Ⓒ Ⓓ
2. Ⓐ Ⓑ Ⓒ Ⓓ
3. Ⓐ Ⓑ Ⓒ Ⓓ
4. Ⓐ Ⓑ Ⓒ Ⓓ
5. Ⓐ Ⓑ Ⓒ Ⓓ

Page 18
1. Ⓐ Ⓑ Ⓒ Ⓓ
2. Ⓐ Ⓑ Ⓒ Ⓓ
3. Ⓐ Ⓑ Ⓒ Ⓓ
4. Ⓐ Ⓑ Ⓒ Ⓓ
5. Ⓐ Ⓑ Ⓒ Ⓓ

Page 19
1. Ⓐ Ⓑ Ⓒ Ⓓ
2. Ⓐ Ⓑ Ⓒ Ⓓ
3. Ⓐ Ⓑ Ⓒ Ⓓ
4. Ⓐ Ⓑ Ⓒ Ⓓ
5. Ⓐ Ⓑ Ⓒ Ⓓ

Page 20
1. Ⓐ Ⓑ Ⓒ Ⓓ
2. Ⓐ Ⓑ Ⓒ Ⓓ
3. Ⓐ Ⓑ Ⓒ Ⓓ
4. Ⓐ Ⓑ Ⓒ Ⓓ
5. Ⓐ Ⓑ Ⓒ Ⓓ

Page 21
1. Ⓐ Ⓑ Ⓒ Ⓓ
2. Ⓐ Ⓑ Ⓒ Ⓓ
3. Ⓐ Ⓑ Ⓒ Ⓓ
4. Ⓐ Ⓑ Ⓒ Ⓓ
5. Ⓐ Ⓑ Ⓒ Ⓓ

Page 22
1. Ⓐ Ⓑ Ⓒ Ⓓ
2. Ⓐ Ⓑ Ⓒ Ⓓ
3. Ⓐ Ⓑ Ⓒ Ⓓ
4. Ⓐ Ⓑ Ⓒ Ⓓ
5. Ⓐ Ⓑ Ⓒ Ⓓ

Page 23
1. Ⓐ Ⓑ Ⓒ Ⓓ
2. Ⓐ Ⓑ Ⓒ Ⓓ
3. Ⓐ Ⓑ Ⓒ Ⓓ
4. Ⓐ Ⓑ Ⓒ Ⓓ
5. Ⓐ Ⓑ Ⓒ Ⓓ

Page 24
1. Ⓐ Ⓑ Ⓒ Ⓓ
2. Ⓐ Ⓑ Ⓒ Ⓓ
3. Ⓐ Ⓑ Ⓒ Ⓓ
4. Ⓐ Ⓑ Ⓒ Ⓓ
5. Ⓐ Ⓑ Ⓒ Ⓓ

Pages 30–31
1. Ⓐ Ⓑ Ⓒ Ⓓ
2. Ⓐ Ⓑ Ⓒ Ⓓ
3. Ⓐ Ⓑ Ⓒ Ⓓ
4. Ⓐ Ⓑ Ⓒ Ⓓ
5. Ⓐ Ⓑ Ⓒ Ⓓ
6. Ⓐ Ⓑ Ⓒ Ⓓ
7. Ⓐ Ⓑ Ⓒ Ⓓ
8. Ⓐ Ⓑ Ⓒ Ⓓ
9. Ⓐ Ⓑ Ⓒ Ⓓ
10. Ⓐ Ⓑ Ⓒ Ⓓ

Page 32
1. Ⓐ Ⓑ Ⓒ Ⓓ
2. Ⓐ Ⓑ Ⓒ Ⓓ
3. Ⓐ Ⓑ Ⓒ Ⓓ
4. Ⓐ Ⓑ Ⓒ Ⓓ
5. Ⓐ Ⓑ Ⓒ Ⓓ

Page 33
1. Ⓐ Ⓑ Ⓒ Ⓓ
2. Ⓐ Ⓑ Ⓒ Ⓓ
3. Ⓐ Ⓑ Ⓒ Ⓓ
4. Ⓐ Ⓑ Ⓒ Ⓓ
5. Ⓐ Ⓑ Ⓒ Ⓓ

Page 34
1. Ⓐ Ⓑ Ⓒ Ⓓ
2. Ⓐ Ⓑ Ⓒ Ⓓ
3. Ⓐ Ⓑ Ⓒ Ⓓ
4. Ⓐ Ⓑ Ⓒ Ⓓ
5. Ⓐ Ⓑ Ⓒ Ⓓ

Page 35
1. Ⓐ Ⓑ Ⓒ Ⓓ
2. Ⓐ Ⓑ Ⓒ Ⓓ
3. Ⓐ Ⓑ Ⓒ Ⓓ
4. Ⓐ Ⓑ Ⓒ Ⓓ
5. Ⓐ Ⓑ Ⓒ Ⓓ

Page 36
1. Ⓐ Ⓑ Ⓒ Ⓓ
2. Ⓐ Ⓑ Ⓒ Ⓓ
3. Ⓐ Ⓑ Ⓒ Ⓓ
4. Ⓐ Ⓑ Ⓒ Ⓓ
5. Ⓐ Ⓑ Ⓒ Ⓓ

Page 37
1. Ⓐ Ⓑ Ⓒ Ⓓ
2. Ⓐ Ⓑ Ⓒ Ⓓ
3. Ⓐ Ⓑ Ⓒ Ⓓ
4. Ⓐ Ⓑ Ⓒ Ⓓ
5. Ⓐ Ⓑ Ⓒ Ⓓ

Page 38
1. Ⓐ Ⓑ Ⓒ Ⓓ
2. Ⓐ Ⓑ Ⓒ Ⓓ
3. Ⓐ Ⓑ Ⓒ Ⓓ
4. Ⓐ Ⓑ Ⓒ Ⓓ
5. Ⓐ Ⓑ Ⓒ Ⓓ

Page 39
1. Ⓐ Ⓑ Ⓒ Ⓓ
2. Ⓐ Ⓑ Ⓒ Ⓓ
3. Ⓐ Ⓑ Ⓒ Ⓓ
4. Ⓐ Ⓑ Ⓒ Ⓓ
5. Ⓐ Ⓑ Ⓒ Ⓓ

Pages 45–46
1. Ⓐ Ⓑ Ⓒ Ⓓ
2. Ⓐ Ⓑ Ⓒ Ⓓ
3. Ⓐ Ⓑ Ⓒ Ⓓ
4. Ⓐ Ⓑ Ⓒ Ⓓ
5. Ⓐ Ⓑ Ⓒ Ⓓ
6. Ⓐ Ⓑ Ⓒ Ⓓ
7. Ⓐ Ⓑ Ⓒ Ⓓ
8. Ⓐ Ⓑ Ⓒ Ⓓ
9. Ⓐ Ⓑ Ⓒ Ⓓ
10. Ⓐ Ⓑ Ⓒ Ⓓ

Page 47
1. Ⓐ Ⓑ Ⓒ Ⓓ
2. Ⓐ Ⓑ Ⓒ Ⓓ
3. Ⓐ Ⓑ Ⓒ Ⓓ
4. Ⓐ Ⓑ Ⓒ Ⓓ
5. Ⓐ Ⓑ Ⓒ Ⓓ

Page 48
1. Ⓐ Ⓑ Ⓒ Ⓓ
2. Ⓐ Ⓑ Ⓒ Ⓓ
3. Ⓐ Ⓑ Ⓒ Ⓓ
4. Ⓐ Ⓑ Ⓒ Ⓓ
5. Ⓐ Ⓑ Ⓒ Ⓓ

Page 49
1. Ⓐ Ⓑ Ⓒ Ⓓ
2. Ⓐ Ⓑ Ⓒ Ⓓ
3. Ⓐ Ⓑ Ⓒ Ⓓ
4. Ⓐ Ⓑ Ⓒ Ⓓ
5. Ⓐ Ⓑ Ⓒ Ⓓ

Page 50
1. Ⓐ Ⓑ Ⓒ Ⓓ
2. Ⓐ Ⓑ Ⓒ Ⓓ
3. Ⓐ Ⓑ Ⓒ Ⓓ
4. Ⓐ Ⓑ Ⓒ Ⓓ
5. Ⓐ Ⓑ Ⓒ Ⓓ

Page 51
1. Ⓐ Ⓑ Ⓒ Ⓓ
2. Ⓐ Ⓑ Ⓒ Ⓓ
3. Ⓐ Ⓑ Ⓒ Ⓓ
4. Ⓐ Ⓑ Ⓒ Ⓓ
5. Ⓐ Ⓑ Ⓒ Ⓓ

Page 52
1. Ⓐ Ⓑ Ⓒ Ⓓ
2. Ⓐ Ⓑ Ⓒ Ⓓ
3. Ⓐ Ⓑ Ⓒ Ⓓ
4. Ⓐ Ⓑ Ⓒ Ⓓ
5. Ⓐ Ⓑ Ⓒ Ⓓ

Page 53
1. Ⓐ Ⓑ Ⓒ Ⓓ
2. Ⓐ Ⓑ Ⓒ Ⓓ
3. Ⓐ Ⓑ Ⓒ Ⓓ
4. Ⓐ Ⓑ Ⓒ Ⓓ
5. Ⓐ Ⓑ Ⓒ Ⓓ

Pages 59–60
1. Ⓐ Ⓑ Ⓒ Ⓓ
2. Ⓐ Ⓑ Ⓒ Ⓓ
3. Ⓐ Ⓑ Ⓒ Ⓓ
4. Ⓐ Ⓑ Ⓒ Ⓓ
5. Ⓐ Ⓑ Ⓒ Ⓓ
6. Ⓐ Ⓑ Ⓒ Ⓓ
7. Ⓐ Ⓑ Ⓒ Ⓓ
8. Ⓐ Ⓑ Ⓒ Ⓓ
9. Ⓐ Ⓑ Ⓒ Ⓓ
10. Ⓐ Ⓑ Ⓒ Ⓓ

Page 61
1. Ⓐ Ⓑ Ⓒ Ⓓ
2. Ⓐ Ⓑ Ⓒ Ⓓ
3. Ⓐ Ⓑ Ⓒ Ⓓ
4. Ⓐ Ⓑ Ⓒ Ⓓ
5. Ⓐ Ⓑ Ⓒ Ⓓ

Page 62
1. Ⓐ Ⓑ Ⓒ Ⓓ
2. Ⓐ Ⓑ Ⓒ Ⓓ
3. Ⓐ Ⓑ Ⓒ Ⓓ
4. Ⓐ Ⓑ Ⓒ Ⓓ
5. Ⓐ Ⓑ Ⓒ Ⓓ

Page 63
1. Ⓐ Ⓑ Ⓒ Ⓓ
2. Ⓐ Ⓑ Ⓒ Ⓓ
3. Ⓐ Ⓑ Ⓒ Ⓓ
4. Ⓐ Ⓑ Ⓒ Ⓓ
5. Ⓐ Ⓑ Ⓒ Ⓓ

Page 64
1. Ⓐ Ⓑ Ⓒ Ⓓ
2. Ⓐ Ⓑ Ⓒ Ⓓ
3. Ⓐ Ⓑ Ⓒ Ⓓ
4. Ⓐ Ⓑ Ⓒ Ⓓ
5. Ⓐ Ⓑ Ⓒ Ⓓ

Page 65
1. Ⓐ Ⓑ Ⓒ Ⓓ
2. Ⓐ Ⓑ Ⓒ Ⓓ
3. Ⓐ Ⓑ Ⓒ Ⓓ
4. Ⓐ Ⓑ Ⓒ Ⓓ
5. Ⓐ Ⓑ Ⓒ Ⓓ

Page 66
1. Ⓐ Ⓑ Ⓒ Ⓓ
2. Ⓐ Ⓑ Ⓒ Ⓓ
3. Ⓐ Ⓑ Ⓒ Ⓓ
4. Ⓐ Ⓑ Ⓒ Ⓓ
5. Ⓐ Ⓑ Ⓒ Ⓓ

Page 67
1. Ⓐ Ⓑ Ⓒ Ⓓ
2. Ⓐ Ⓑ Ⓒ Ⓓ
3. Ⓐ Ⓑ Ⓒ Ⓓ
4. Ⓐ Ⓑ Ⓒ Ⓓ
5. Ⓐ Ⓑ Ⓒ Ⓓ

Page 68
1. Ⓐ Ⓑ Ⓒ Ⓓ
2. Ⓐ Ⓑ Ⓒ Ⓓ
3. Ⓐ Ⓑ Ⓒ Ⓓ
4. Ⓐ Ⓑ Ⓒ Ⓓ
5. Ⓐ Ⓑ Ⓒ Ⓓ

Pages 74–75
1. Ⓐ Ⓑ Ⓒ Ⓓ
2. Ⓐ Ⓑ Ⓒ Ⓓ
3. Ⓐ Ⓑ Ⓒ Ⓓ
4. Ⓐ Ⓑ Ⓒ Ⓓ
5. Ⓐ Ⓑ Ⓒ Ⓓ
6. Ⓐ Ⓑ Ⓒ Ⓓ
7. Ⓐ Ⓑ Ⓒ Ⓓ
8. Ⓐ Ⓑ Ⓒ Ⓓ
9. Ⓐ Ⓑ Ⓒ Ⓓ
10. Ⓐ Ⓑ Ⓒ Ⓓ

Answer Key and Item Analysis

Chapter 1: North Carolina's Geography (pages 1–5)
Lesson 1: Where on Earth Is North Carolina?
1 B [1.0.1]
2 C [1.0.1]
3 A [1.0.1]
4 D [1.0.1]
5 C [1.0.2]

Lesson 2: The Shape of the Land
1 C [1.0.1]
2 A [1.0.1]
3 C [1.0.5]
4 D [2.0.4]
5 B [1.0.2]

Lesson 3: North Carolina's Rivers and Lakes
1 C [1.0.2]
2 C [1.0.2]
3 B [4.0.5]
4 A [1.0.2]
5 A [6.0.3]

Lesson 4: North Carolina's Resources
1 C [6.0.4]
2 B [1.0.1]
3 B [6.0.4]
4 D [6.0.3]
5 D [1.0.4]

Lesson 5: Weather and Climate
1 D
2 C
3 A [1.0.2]
4 C
5 A [7.0.5]

Chapter 2: The Early People of North Carolina (pages 6–9)
Lesson 1: The Earliest People
1 B [2.0.1]
2 B [5.0.2]
3 C [3.0.1]

4 C [2.0.3]
5 A [1.0.4]

Lesson 2: People of the Coastal Plain
1 B [2.0.1]
2 C [2.0.1]
3 D [5.0.3]
4 C [1.0.5]
5 D [1.0.4]

Lesson 3: People of the Piedmont
1 D [5.0.3]
2 C [2.0.4]
3 B [4.0.4]
4 A [3.0.1]
5 D [2.0.1]

Lesson 4: People of the Mountains
1 D [2.0.1]
2 B [1.0.4]
3 C [2.0.3]
4 D [4.0.3]
5 B [2.0.4]

Unit 1: Reading Comprehension Questions (pages 15–16)
1 D [1.0.2; Identify the Main Idea and Supporting Details]
2 B [1.0.2; Categorize]
3 A [1.0.1; Compare and Contrast]
4 A [1.0.1; Identify Fact and Opinion]
5 B [1.0.1; Sequence]
6 D [1.0.2; Make Inferences]
7 C [1.0.5; Generalize]
8 D [2.0.1; Summarize]
9 A [2.0.1; Identify the Main Idea and Supporting Details]
10 B [2.0.1; Make Inferences]

Chapter 3: The Coastal Plain Region Long Ago (pages 17–21)
Lesson 1: Explorers and Settlers of the Coastal Plain
1 B [2.0.2]
2 D [3.0.2]

3 C [1.0.5]
4 A [3.0.3]
5 A [3.0.3]

Lesson 2: Settling near Albemarle Sound
1 D [3.0.2]
2 C [4.0.4]
3 B [2.0.2]
4 B [3.0.5]
5 B [4.0.2]

Lesson 3: Colonists Face Challenges
1 C [2.0.4]
2 B [2.0.3]
3 A [3.0.1]
4 C [2.0.1]
5 D [7.0.1]

Lesson 4: Settling near the Cape Fear River
1 C [3.0.2]
2 A [1.0.3]
3 D [2.0.3]
4 B [6.0.4]
5 D [3.0.1]

Lesson 5: The American Revolution
1 B [6.0.8]
2 C [3.0.5]
3 B [3.0.2]
4 A [4.0.3]
5 D [3.0.2]

Chapter 4: The Coastal Plain Region Today (pages 22–24)
Lesson 1: Living in the Coastal Plain
1 C [1.0.3]
2 D [7.0.2]
3 A [7.0.3]
4 B [1.0.3]
5 C [6.0.2]

Lesson 2: Working in the Coastal Plain
1 C [6.0.7]
2 B [6.0.4]
3 D [1.0.4]
4 B [1.0.3]
5 A [6.0.1]

Lesson 3: Coastal Life
1 A [1.0.1]
2 C [1.0.1]
3 C
4 D [7.0.5]
5 A [5.0.1]

Unit 2: Reading Comprehension Questions (pages 30–31)
1 A [3.0.5; Identify the Main Idea and Supporting Details]
2 C [3.0.5; Cause and Effect]
3 B [3.0.5; Make Inferences]
4 D [3.0.4; Summarize]
5 B [3.0.5; Generalize]
6 C [3.0.5; Draw Conclusions]
7 D [3.0.5; Identify the Main Idea and Supporting Details]
8 C [1.0.2; Identify the Main Idea and Supporting Details]
9 D [6.0.7; Compare and Contrast]
10 C [Predict a Likely Outcome]

Chapter 5: The Piedmont Region Long Ago (pages 32–36)
Lesson 1: Settling the Backcountry
1 C [1.0.1]
2 B [1.0.5]
3 A [3.0.4]
4 D [2.0.4]
5 B [4.0.2]

Lesson 2: From a Colony to a State
1 B [4.0.5]
2 D [3.0.2]
3 A [4.0.3]
4 C [6.0.3]
5 C [6.0.6]

Lesson 3: Conflicting Views
1 D [3.0.1]
2 C [4.0.2]
3 B [4.0.5]
4 A [2.0.3]
5 B [3.0.2]

Lesson 4: North Carolina in the Civil War
1 B [2.0.3]
2 D [3.0.2]

3 D [2.0.3]
4 C [3.0.2]
5 B [4.0.5]
Lesson 5: Growth and Industry
1 B [6.0.2]
2 A [7.0.5]
3 C [7.0.2]
4 C [6.0.2]
5 D [6.0.3]

Chapter 6: The Piedmont Region Today (pages 37–39)
Lesson 1: The Piedmont Urban Crescent
1 A [1.0.4]
2 D [1.0.3]
3 C [7.0.3]
4 B [1.0.3]
5 C [4.0.2]
Lesson 2: Piedmont Industries Change
1 D [6.0.4]
2 B [7.0.1]
3 C [7.0.5]
4 A [7.0.3]
5 C [7.0.5]
Lesson 3: Life in the Piedmont
1 B [5.0.1]
2 C [5.0.1]
3 B
4 A [5.0.3]
5 D [5.0.2]
Unit 3: Reading Comprehension Questions (pages 45–46)
1 B [1.0.5; Identify the Main Idea and Supporting Details]
2 C [4.0.2; Compare and Contrast]
3 B [4.0.2; Sequence]
4 D [3.0.5; Cause and Effect]
5 A [6.0.2; Make Inferences]
6 B [3.0.2; Summarize]
7 C [3.0.2; Sequence]
8 A [3.0.1; Compare and Contrast]
9 D [6.0.2; Identify Fact and Opinion]
10 C [5.0.3; Sequence]

Chapter 7: The Mountain Region Long Ago (pages 47–50)
Lesson 1: Settling the Western Mountains
1 C [1.0.5]
2 D [4.0.5]
3 B [1.0.4]
4 C [1.0.3]
5 B [3.0.4]
Lesson 2: Life on the Mountain Frontier
1 C [3.0.2]
2 A [1.0.3]
3 B [3.0.1]
4 D [5.0.3]
5 A [3.0.2]
Lesson 3: The Cherokees in North Carolina
1 D [2.0.1]
2 B [3.0.2]
3 A [2.0.3]
4 C [1.0.5]
5 B [2.0.1]
Lesson 4: Growth in the Mountain Region
1 D [1.0.2]
2 B [6.0.1]
3 B [6.0.2]
4 A [7.0.3]
5 D [1.0.1]

Chapter 8: The Mountain Region Today (pages 51–53)
Lesson 1: Living in the Mountain Region
1 C [4.0.1]
2 A [5.0.2]
3 B [5.0.1]
4 A [5.0.3]
5 D [2.0.3]
Lesson 2: Working in the Mountain Region
1 B [6.0.4]
2 C [1.0.4]
3 D [6.0.3]
4 A [6.0.4]
5 B [6.0.1]

Lesson 3: A View from the Mountains
  1 **C** [1.0.1]
  2 **D** [2.0.1]
  3 **A** [4.0.5]
  4 **B** [1.0.3]
  5 **A** [5.0.1]

Unit 4: Reading Comprehension Questions (pages 59–60)
  1 **C** [3.0.5; Identify the Main Idea and Supporting Details]
  2 **B** [2.0.1; Identify Fact and Opinion]
  3 **A** [2.0.1; Draw Conclusions]
  4 **D** [2.0.1; Cause and Effect]
  5 **A** [3.0.2; Make Inferences]
  6 **B** [3.0.1; Draw Conclusions]
  7 **C** [6.0.1; Identify the Main Idea and Supporting Details]
  8 **D** [6.0.1; Compare and Contrast]
  9 **C** [6.0.1; Cause and Effect]
 10 **B** [7.0.3; Sequence]

Chapter 9: North Carolina: The Twentieth Century and Beyond (pages 61–63)
Lesson 1: A New Century Brings Change
  1 **D** [1.04, 7.0.5]
  2 **D** [4.0.5]
  3 **B** [1.0.4, 6.0.3, 6.0.6]
  4 **C** [3.0.2, 4.0.3]
  5 **A** [1.0.1, 1.0.4, 6.0.3, 7.0.1, 7.0.3]

Lesson 2: World Events Affect North Carolina
  1 **B** [1.0.3]
  2 **D** [4.0.3, 6.0.2, 6.0.5]
  3 **C** [6.0.1, 6.0.2, 6.0.5]
  4 **A** [4.0.5]
  5 **C** [6.0.3]

Lesson 3: North Carolina After World War II
  1 **B** [6.0.2]
  2 **C** [2.0.3]
  3 **D** [4.0.1]
  4 **D** [4.0.5]
  5 **A** [4.0.3]

Chapter 10: North Carolina Today (pages 64–68)
Lesson 1: Into the Twenty-First Century
  1 **C** [1.0.3]
  2 **B** [2.0.2]
  3 **B** [5.0.3]
  4 **D** [2.0.3, 5.0.1]
  5 **A** [6.0.7, 6.0.8]

Lesson 2: Government in North Carolina Today
  1 **B** [3.0.2]
  2 **C** [4.0.4]
  3 **B** [6.0.6]
  4 **A** [4.0.4]
  5 **D** [4.0.4]

Lesson 3: Local Governments
  1 **D** [4.0.4, 6.0.6]
  2 **C** [4.0.4]
  3 **A** [4.0.5]
  4 **B** [4.0.4, 6.0.6]
  5 **C** [4.0.4]

Lesson 4: The National Government
  1 **B** [4.0.4]
  2 **C** [4.0.4]
  3 **B** [4.0.4]
  4 **D** [4.0.5]
  5 **A** [4.0.5]

Lesson 5: North Carolina Citizenship
  1 **C**
  2 **D** [4.0.2, 4.0.3]
  3 **B** [4.0.3]
  4 **A** [4.0.4]
  5 **D** [4.0.3]

Unit 5: Reading Comprehension Questions (pages 74–75)

1. **B** [1.0.3, 4.0.5, 7.0.1, 7.0.2, 7.0.3; Categorize]
2. **D** [1.0.1, 1.0.4; Generalize]
3. **C** [Sequence]
4. **A** [4.0.3; Identify the Main Idea and Supporting Details]
5. **B** [6.0.2; Cause and Efect]
6. **C** [3.0.1, 4.0.3; Identify Fact and Opinion]
7. **A** [6.0.8; Summarize]
8. **D** [4.0.4; Compare and Contrast]
9. **A** [4.0.4; Generalize]
10. **B** [4.0.3, 4.0.4; Draw Conclusions]

North Carolina GRADE 4 Standards

COMPETENCY GOAL 1	PAGES (ITEMS)
The learner will apply the five themes of geography to North Carolina and its people.	
Objectives	
1.0.1 Locate, in absolute and relative terms, major landforms, bodies of water and natural resources in North Carolina.	1 (1, 2, 3, 4), 2 (1, 2), 4 (2), 15 (3, 4, 5), 24 (1, 2), 32 (1), 50 (5), 53 (1), 61 (5), 74 (2)
1.0.2 Describe and compare physical and cultural characteristics of the regions.	1 (5), 2 (5), 3 (1, 2, 4), 5 (3), 15 (1, 2), 16 (6), 31 (8), 50 (1), 52 (4)
1.0.3 Suggest some influences that location has on life in North Carolina such as major cities, recreation areas, industry, and farms.	20 (2), 22 (1, 4), 23 (4), 37 (2, 4), 47 (4), 48 (2), 53 (4), 62 (1), 64 (1), 74 (1)
1.0.4 Evaluate ways the people of North Carolina used, modified, and adapted to the physical environment, past and present.	4 (5), 6 (5), 7 (5), 9 (2), 23 (3), 37 (1), 47 (3), 52 (2), 61 (1, 3, 5), 74 (2)
1.0.5 Assess human movement as it relates to the physical environment.	2 (3), 7 (4), 16 (7), 17 (3), 32 (2), 45 (1), 47 (1), 49 (4)
COMPETENCY GOAL 2	
The learner will examine the importance of the role of ethnic groups and examine the multiple roles they have played in the development of North Carolina.	
2.0.1 Locate and describe American Indians in North Carolina, past and present.	6 (1), 7 (1, 2), 8 (5), 9 (1), 16 (8, 9, 10), 19 (4), 49 (1, 5), 53 (2), 59 (2, 3, 4)
2.0.2 Trace the growth and development of immigration to North Carolina, over time from Europe, Asia, and Latin America.	17 (1), 18 (3), 64 (2)
2.0.3 Describe the similarities and differences among people of North Carolina, past and present.	6 (4), 9 (3), 19 (2), 20 (3), 34 (4), 35 (1, 3), 49 (3), 51 (5), 63 (2), 64 (4)
2.0.4 Describe how different ethnic groups have influenced culture, customs and history of North Carolina.	2 (4), 8 (2), 9 (5), 19 (1), 32 (4)
COMPETENCY GOAL 3	
The learner will trace the history of colonization in North Carolina and evaluate its significance for diverse people's ideas.	
3.0.1 Assess changes in ways of living over time and determine whether the changes are primarily political, economic, or social.	6 (3), 8 (4), 19 (3), 20 (5), 34 (1), 46 (8), 48 (3), 60 (6), 75 (6)
3.0.2 Identify people, symbols, events, and documents associated with North Carolina's history.	17 (2), 18 (1), 20 (1), 21 (3, 5), 33 (2), 34 (5), 35 (2, 4), 46 (6, 7), 48 (1, 5), 49 (2), 60 (5), 61 (4), 65 (1)
3.0.3 Examine the Lost Colony and explain its importance in the settlement of North Carolina.	17 (4, 5)
3.0.4 Compare and contrast ways in which people, goods, and ideas moved in the past with their movement today.	30 (4), 32 (3), 47 (5)
3.0.5 Describe the political and social history of colonial North Carolina and analyze its influence on the state today.	18 (4), 21 (2), 30 (1, 2, 3, 5), 31 (6, 7), 32 (3), 45 (4), 59 (1)

COMPETENCY GOAL 4	
The learner will analyze social and political institutions in North Carolina such as government, education, religion, and family and how they structure society, influence behavior, and response to human needs.	
4.0.1 Assess and evaluate the importance of regional diversity on the development of economic, social, and political institutions in North Carolina.	51 (1), 63 (3)
4.0.2 Identify religious groups that have influenced life in North Carolina and assess the impact of their beliefs.	18 (5), 32 (5), 34 (2), 37 (5), 45 (2, 3), 68 (2)
4.0.3 Explain the importance of responsible citizenship and identify ways North Carolinians can participate in civic affairs.	9 (4), 21 (4), 33 (3), 61 (4), 62 (2), 63 (5), 68 (2, 3, 5), 74 (4), 75 (6, 10)
4.0.4 Examine ways North Carolinians govern themselves and identify major government authorities at the local and state level.	8 (3), 18 (2), 65 (2, 4, 5), 66 (1, 2, 4, 5), 67 (1, 2, 3), 68 (4), 75 (8, 9, 10)
4.0.5 Identify and assess the role of prominent persons in North Carolina, past and present.	3 (3), 33 (1), 34 (3), 35 (5), 47 (2), 53 (3), 61 (2), 62 (4), 63 (4), 66 (3), 67 (4, 5), 74 (1)

COMPETENCY GOAL 5	
The learner will examine the impact of various cultural groups on North Carolina.	
5.0.1 Explain different celebrated holidays, special days, and cultural traditions in North Carolina communities.	24 (5), 39 (1, 2), 51 (3), 53 (5), 64 (4)
5.0.2 Describe traditional art music and craft forms in North Carolina.	6 (2), 39 (5), 51 (2)
5.0.3 Describe and compare the cultural characteristics of regions within North Carolina and evaluate their significance.	7 (3), 8 (1), 39 (4), 46 (10), 48 (4), 51 (4), 64 (3)

COMPETENCY GOAL 6	
The learner will evaluate how North Carolinians apply basic economic principles within the community, state, and nation.	
6.0.1 Explain the relationship between unlimited wants and limited resources.	23 (5), 50 (2), 52 (5), 60 (7, 8, 9), 62 (3)
6.0.2 Analyze the choices and opportunity cost involved in economic decisions.	22 (5), 36 (1, 4), 45 (5), 46 (9), 50 (3), 62 (2, 3), 63 (1), 74 (5)
6.0.3 Categorize the state's resources as natural, human, or capital.	3 (5), 4 (4), 33 (4), 36 (5), 52 (3), 61 (3, 5), 62 (5)
6.0.4 Assess how the state's natural resources are being used.	4 (1, 3), 20 (4), 23 (2), 38 (1), 52 (1, 4)
6.0.5 Recognize that money can be used for spending, saving, and paying taxes.	62 (2, 3)
6.0.6 Analyze the relationship between government services and taxes.	33 (5), 61 (3), 65 (3), 66 (1, 4)
6.0.7 Describe the ways North Carolina specializes in economic activity and the relationship between specialization and interdependence.	23 (1), 31 (9), 64 (5)
6.0.8 Cite examples of interdependence in North Carolina's economy and evaluate the significance of economic relationships with other states and nations.	21 (1), 64 (5), 75 (7)

COMPETENCY GOAL 7	
The learner will recognize how technology influences change within North Carolina.	
7.0.1 Cite examples from North Carolina's history of the impact of technology.	19 (5), 38 (2), 61 (5), 74 (1)
7.0.2 Analyze the effect of technology on North Carolina's citizens, past and present.	22 (2), 36 (3), 74 (1)
7.0.3 Explain how technology changed and influenced the movement of people, goods, and ideas over time.	22 (3), 37 (3), 38 (4), 50 (4), 60 (10), 61 (5), 74 (1)
7.0.4 Analyze the effect of technology on North Carolina citizens today.	
7.0.5 Identify the advantages and disadvantages of technology in the lives of North Carolinians.	5 (5), 24 (4), 36 (2), 38 (3, 5), 61 (1)

Correlation Chart

Test Preparation ■ 13